Scrappy Fat Quarter Quilts

Favorite Projects from
Fons&Porter

Scrappy Fat Quarter Quilts: Favorite Projects from Fons & Porter
© 2014 Fons & Porter

FONS & PORTER STAFF
Editors-in-Chief Marianne Fons and Liz Porter

Editor Jean Nolte
Managing Editor Debra Finan
Associate Editor Diane Tomlinson
Technical Writer Kristine Peterson

Art Director Tony Jacobson
Graphic Designer Kelsey Wolfswinkel

Sewing Specialist Colleen Tauke

Contributing Photographers Craig Anderson, Kathryn Gamble, Rick Lozier,
Dean Tanner
Contributing Photo Assistants Mary Mouw, DeElda Wittmack

Publisher Kristi Loeffelholz

Fons & Porter
54 Court
Winterset, IA 50273
FonsandPorter.com

Produced by:
Martingale®
19021 120th Ave. NE, Ste. 102
Bothell, WA 98011-9511 USA
ShopMartingale.com

Printed in China
19 18 17 16 15 14   8 7 6 5 4 3 2 1

Library of Congress Cataloging-in-Publication Data
is available upon request

ISBN: 978-1-60468-569-5

Contents

Introduction

Quilters love fat quarters, and it's easy to understand why. Beautifully displayed in bundles and baskets—often right at the checkout counter—these tempting little bits of fabric are irresistible! They're fun to collect and even more fun to use, and what better place to use them than a scrap quilt?

We're delighted to present this outstanding collection of favorite scrap-quilt projects, all of them made with fat quarters. You'll find time-honored traditional patterns as well as fresh, modern designs. Whether you're looking for a new bed quilt, cozy lap quilt, or striking wall hanging, you'll find the perfect project here. Our trademarked *Sew Easy* lessons will guide you through any project-specific special techniques.

Fat quarters and scrap quilts: what a happy combination!

Happy quilting,

Marianne + Liz

Monkey Business

Sometimes, less is more. Evelyn Young's quilt is beautiful in its simplicity.
The authentic naturally-dyed indigo fabrics from South Africa add to its beauty.

Size: 54" × 66"

Blocks: 32 (6") Monkey Wrench blocks

MATERIALS

12 fat quarters** assorted dark prints
12 fat quarters* assorted light prints
⅝ yard binding fabric
3½ yards backing fabric
Twin-size quilt batting
** Shweshwe fat quarter = 18" × 18"
*fat quarter = 18" × 20"

NOTE: Dark fabrics in the quilt shown are Shweshwe prints from South Africa by Marula Imports. Authentic Shweshwe is 36" wide. It must be washed prior to use to remove excess dye and starch. Find washing instructions and more about Shweshwe on page 9.

Cutting

Measurements include ¼" seam allowances.

From each dark print fat quarter, cut:

- 2 (6½"-wide) strips. From 1 strip, cut 2 (6½") A squares. From 1 strip, cut 1 (6½") A square and 6 (2⅞") squares. Cut 2⅞" squares in half diagonally to make 12 half-square C triangles.
- 2 (1½"-wide) strips for strip sets.

From each light print fat quarter, cut:

- 2 (6½"-wide) strips. From 1 strip, cut 2 (6½") A squares and 3 (2½") B squares. From 1 strip, cut 1 (6½") A square and 6 (2⅞") squares. Cut 2⅞" squares in half diagonally to make 12 half-square C triangles.
- 2 (1½"-wide) strips for strip sets.

From binding fabric, cut:

- 7 (2¼"-wide) strips for binding.

Block Assembly

1. Join 1 dark print strip and 1 light print strip as shown in *Strip Set Diagram*. Make 2 matching strip sets. Make 12 pairs of matching strip sets. From each pair of strip sets, cut 12 (2½"-wide) segments (you will have a few extra).

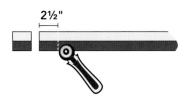

Strip Set Diagram

2. Select 1 matching set of 4 strip set segments, 4 dark print C triangles, 4 light print C triangles, and 1 light print B square.

3. Join 1 light print C triangle and 1 dark print C triangle as shown in *Triangle-Square Diagrams*. Make 4 triangle-squares.

Triangle-Square Diagrams

4. Lay out triangle-squares, strip set segments, and B square as shown in *Block Assembly Diagram*. Join into rows; join rows to complete 1 Monkey Wrench block *(Block Diagram)*. Make 32 Monkey Wrench blocks.

Block Assembly Diagram

Block Diagram

Quilt Assembly

1. Lay out blocks and A squares as shown in *Quilt Top Assembly Diagram*.

2. Join into rows; join rows to complete quilt top.

Finishing

1. Divide backing into 2 (1¾-yard) lengths. Join panels lengthwise. Seam will run horizontally.

2. Layer backing, batting, and quilt top; baste. Quilt as desired. Quilt shown was quilted with a fleur-de-lis design in the light A squares, and with parallel straight lines in the dark A (border) squares *(Quilting Diagram)*.

3. Join 2¼"-wide binding strips into 1 continuous piece for straight-grain French-fold binding. Add binding to quilt.

Quilt Top Assembly Diagram

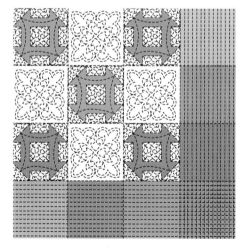

Quilting Diagram

Washing Instructions

1. Serge or zigzag fabric edges before washing.

2. Wash in cold water using non-phosphate detergent such as Orvus, Ivory, or Dreft.

3. High water level ensures water will adequately circulate through the fabric.

4. Rinse in cold water. Run fabric through additional rinse cycles until water runs clear.

5. Dry flat or tumble dry. Shweshwe shrinks when machine dried, so be sure to tumble dry for any projects that will be washed later.

6. Press using cotton setting on iron.

About Shweshwe Fabric

Shweshwe is manufactured in South Africa by Da Gama Textiles—the only known producer of traditional indigo-dyed discharge printed fabric in the world. The intricate indigo, white, chocolate brown, and red prints remain in steady demand for traditional African clothing and tourism products, and now for quiltmaking in America.

It is believed by some that the name Shweshwe comes from the swishing sound the fabric makes when the wearer walks. However, according to Da Gama Textiles' history, the cloth was gifted to, and named for, King Moshoeshoe. By association with the king, the cloth was called shoeshoe, and eventually shweshwe.

Shweshwe fabric is 36" wide, and is dyed using natural indigo from many different plants. Indigo itself is not a true dye, but when used, produces a chemical reaction between the fabric and the agent. When fabric is pulled out of the dye pot, the agent oxidizes with air to produce the beautiful blue color.

To read more about Shweshwe, go to:

indigo.cottoninthecabin.com

Milky Way

Milky Way is a tessellating pattern, which means it is tiled or interlocking. Although you can clearly see stars, there is no actual star block in this quilt. The stars appear only after you join the units together. Trade 2½"-wide and 4½"-wide strips with your friends for more fabric variety.

Size: 64" × 80"

MATERIALS

- 18 fat quarters* assorted light shirting prints
- 16 fat quarters* assorted dark prints in black, purple, green, blue, gold, brown, and pink
- Fons & Porter Half & Quarter Ruler (optional)
- ⅝ yard red print for binding
- 5 yards backing fabric
- Twin-size quilt batting

*fat quarter = 18" × 20"

Cutting

Measurements include ¼" seam allowances. Instructions are written for using the Fons & Porter Half & Quarter Ruler. If not using this ruler, follow cutting NOTES.

From assorted light print fat quarters, cut a total of:

- 25 (4½"-wide) strips. From strips, cut 24 (4½") A squares and 110 half-square B triangles.

  NOTE: If not using the Fons & Porter Half & Quarter Ruler, cut a total of 19 (4⅞"-wide) strips. From strips, cut 55 (4⅞") squares. Cut squares in half diagonally to make 110 half-square B triangles.

- 6 (4½"-wide) strips. From strips, cut 24 (4½") A squares.
- 53 (2½"-wide) strips for strip sets.

From assorted dark print fat quarters, cut a total of:

- 25 (4½"-wide) strips. From strips, cut 24 (4½") A squares and 110 half-square B triangles.

NOTE: If not using the Fons & Porter Half & Quarter Ruler, cut a total of 19 (4⅞"-wide) strips and 6 (4½"-wide) strips. From (4⅞"-wide) strips, cut 55 (4⅞") squares. Cut squares in half diagonally to make 110 half-square B triangles. From 4½"-wide strips, cut 24 (4½") A squares.

- 38 (2½"-wide) strips for strip sets.

From red print, cut:

- 8 (2¼"-wide) strips for binding.

Quilt Center Assembly

1. Join 1 light print (2½"-wide) strip and 1 dark print (2½"-wide) strip as shown in *Strip Set Diagram*. Make 38 strip sets. From strip sets, cut 262 (2½"-wide) segments.

2½"

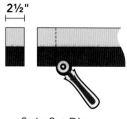

Strip Set Diagram

2. Join 2 segments as shown in *Four Patch Unit Diagrams*. Make 131 Four Patch Units.

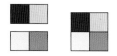

Four Patch Unit Diagrams

3. Join 1 light print B triangle and 1 dark print B triangle as shown in *Triangle-Square Diagrams*. Make 110 triangle-squares.

Triangle-Square Diagrams

4. Lay out 63 Four Patch Units, triangle-squares, and light and dark print A squares as shown in *Quilt Top Assembly Diagram*. Join into rows; join rows to complete quilt center.

Pieced Border Assembly

1. Join remaining light print 2½"-wide strips end to end to make one long strip. From strip, cut 2 (2½" × 68½") side inner borders and 2 (2½" × 56½") top and bottom inner borders.

2. Lay out 18 Four Patch Units as shown in *Quilt Top Assembly Diagram*. Join to complete 1 side outer border. Make 2 side outer borders.

3. In the same manner, join 16 Four Patch Units to make top outer border. Repeat for bottom outer border.

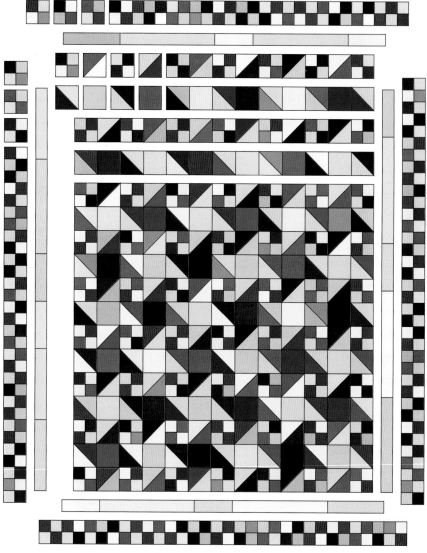

Quilt Top Assembly Diagram

Quilt Assembly

1. Add side inner borders to quilt center. Add top and bottom inner borders to quilt.

2. Repeat for pieced outer borders.

Finishing

1. Divide backing into 2 (2½-yard) lengths. Cut 1 piece in half lengthwise to make 2 narrow panels.

Join 1 narrow panel to each side of wider panel; press seam allowances toward narrow panels.

2. Layer backing, batting, and quilt top; baste. Quilt as desired. Quilt shown was quilted with a Baptist Fan design *(Quilting Diagram)*.

3. Join 2¼"-wide red print strips into 1 continuous piece for straight-grain French-fold binding. Add binding to quilt.

Quilting Diagram

Candy Store

Gray serves as a neutral when combined with bright prints to give this scrappy throw a modern look. For even more variety, trade 1½"-wide bright strips with friends.

Size: 52" × 69"

Blocks: 12 (16") blocks

MATERIALS

18 fat quarters* assorted prints in pink, turquoise, green, orange, blue, purple, and gray for blocks

1½ yards gray solid for sashing, border, and binding

3½ yards backing fabric

Twin-size quilt batting

*fat quarter = 18" × 20"

Cutting

Measurements include ¼" seam allowances. Border strips are exact length needed. You may want to cut them longer to allow for piecing variations.

From turquoise print fat quarter, cut:

• 2 (4½"-wide) strips. From strips, cut 6 (4½") A squares.

From pink print fat quarter, cut:

• 2 (4½"-wide) strips. From strips, cut 6 (4½") A squares.

From remainders of turquoise and pink fat quarters and remaining fat quarters, cut a total of:

• 176 (1½"-wide) strips for strip sets.

From gray solid, cut:

• 7 (2¼"-wide) strips for binding.

• 22 (1½"-wide) strips. From 11 strips, cut 8 (1½" × 16½") vertical sashing strips, 24 (1½" × 6½") C rectangles, and 24 (1½" × 4½") B rectangles. Piece remaining strips to make 2 (1½" × 67½") side borders, 2 (1½" × 52½") top and bottom borders, and 3 (1½" × 50½") horizontal sashing strips.

Block Assembly

1. Referring to *Strip Sets* on page 60, join 6 assorted print strips as shown in *Strip Set #1 Diagram*. Make 8 Strip Set #1. From strip sets, cut 24 (5½"-wide) #1 segments.

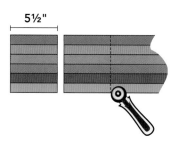

5½"

Strip Set #1 Diagram

Sew Smart™

Measure the height of your strip set. Strip Set #1 should measure exactly 6½". If it is not 6½", adjust seams as needed. Strip Set #2 should measure exactly 16½".
—Marianne

2. Join 16 assorted print strips as shown in *Strip Set #2 Diagram*. Make 8 Strip Set #2. From strip sets, cut 24 (5½"-wide) #2 segments.

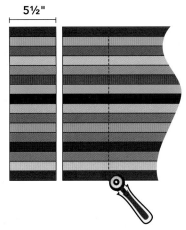

5½"

Strip Set #2 Diagram

3. Join 1 turquoise print A square, 2 gray B rectangles, and 2 gray C rectangles as shown in *Block Center Diagrams*. Make 6 turquoise Block Centers. In the same manner, make 6 pink Block Centers.

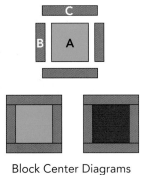

Block Center Diagrams

4. Lay out 1 Block Center, 2 #1 segments, and 2 #2 segments as shown in *Block Assembly Diagram*. Join into rows; join rows to complete 1 block *(Block Diagram)*. Make 12 blocks.

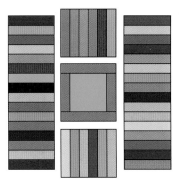

Block Assembly Diagram

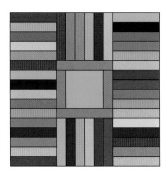

Block Diagram

Quilt Top Assembly Diagram

Quilt Assembly

1. Lay out blocks and sashing strips as shown in *Quilt Top Assembly Diagram*. Join into rows; join rows to complete quilt center.

2. Add gray side borders to quilt center. Add gray top and bottom borders to quilt.

Finishing

1. Divide backing into 2 (1¾-yard) lengths. Join panels lengthwise. Seam will run horizontally.

2. Layer backing, batting, and quilt top; baste. Quilt as desired. Quilt shown was quilted with concentric squares *(Quilting Diagram)*.

3. Join 2¼"-wide gray strips into 1 continuous piece for straight-grain French-fold binding. Add binding to quilt.

Quilting Diagram

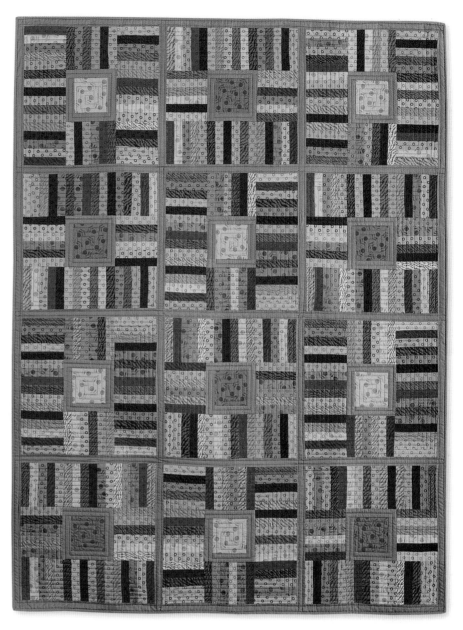

Sparkle Punch

This quilt is fun to make—you'll put your design wall to good use.
The wonkiness of the star points and variety of prints really make the stars sparkle.
Designer Elizabeth Hartman says, "It's my interpretation of the interlocking-star trend."

Size: 60" × 72"

MATERIALS

20 fat quarters* assorted prints in pink,
    teal, black, gray, purple, and brown
    for stars
3¾ yards gray solid for background
⅝ yard brown print for binding
4 yards backing fabric
Twin-size quilt batting
*fat quarter = 18" × 20"

Cutting

Measurements include ¼" seam
allowances.

From fat quarters, cut a total of:

• 80 sets of 5 (3½") squares. Set aside
  1 square of each set to be used
  for star centers. Cut remaining
  squares in half diagonally to make
  80 sets of 8 half-square triangles for
  Whole Stars *(Whole Star Diagram)*.

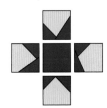

Whole Star Diagram

• 14 sets of 4 (3½") squares. Set aside
  1 square of each set to be used
  for star centers. Cut remaining
  squares in half diagonally to make

14 sets of 6 half-square triangles for
Three-Quarter Stars *(Three-Quarter
Star Diagram)*.

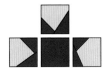

Three-Quarter Star Diagram

• 2 sets of 3 (3½") squares. Set aside 1
  square of each set to be used
  for star centers. Cut remaining
  squares in half diagonally to make
  2 sets of 4 half-square triangles for
  Half Stars *(Half Star Diagram)*.

Half Star Diagram

• 18 single (3½") squares. Cut squares
  in half diagonally to make 18 sets of

2 half-square triangles for Quarter Stars *(Quarter Star Diagram)*.

Quarter Star Diagram

NOTE: The partial stars will be around the edges of the quilt, so make sure they're not all the same fabric or color.

From gray solid, cut:

• 35 (3½"-wide) strips. From strips, cut 384 (3½") squares.

From brown print, cut:

• 8 (2¼"-wide) strips for binding.

Star Point Assembly

1. Referring to *Star Point Unit Diagrams*, place 1 print triangle atop 1 gray square, right sides facing. Stitch with a ¼" seam allowance across corner. Press open to reveal triangle. Trim gray square ¼" beyond stitching. Repeat for adjacent corner using a matching triangle.

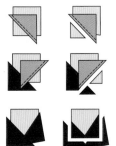

Star Point Unit Diagrams

Sew Smart™

The star points are wonky. Place print triangles on gray squares at varying angles. Just be sure that when triangle is pressed open, it covers corner of gray square underneath. Then trim corner of gray square. —Marianne

2. Trim square to 3½" to complete 1 Star Point Unit. Make 384 Star Point Units.

Quilt Assembly

1. Lay out Star Point Units and star center squares as shown in *Quilt Top Assembly Diagram*.

2. Join into sections; join sections to complete quilt top.

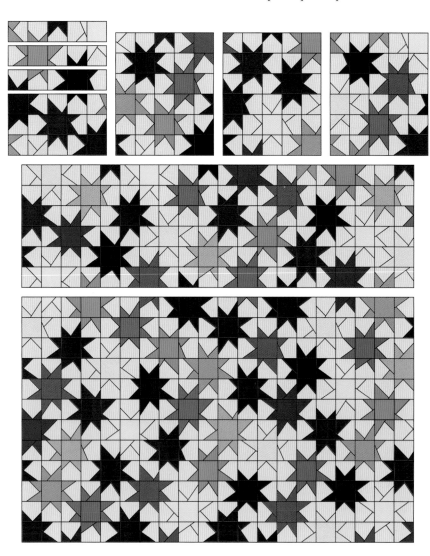

Quilt Top Assembly Diagram

Finishing

1. Divide backing into 2 (2-yard) lengths. Join panels lengthwise. Seam will run horizontally.

2. Layer backing, batting, and quilt top; baste. Quilt as desired. Quilt shown was quilted with an allover zigzag design *(Quilting Diagram)*.

3. Join 2¼"-wide brown print strips into 1 continuous piece for straight-grain French-fold binding. Add binding to quilt.

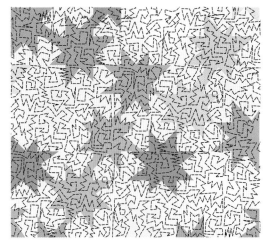

Quilting Diagram

QUILT DESIGNED AND MADE BY **Liz Porter**

HAND QUILTED BY **Ada, Katie, and Vera Troyer and Mary Yoder**

Snowball

"I made this quilt after a block swap with a few friends. We used reproductions fabrics for our quilts because they're our favorites, and limited our color scheme to red, blue, black, and gray for the dark fabrics and shirting prints for the light fabrics. The use of many different prints makes it look like a vintage quilt." —Liz

Size: 83" × 95"

Blocks: 168 (6") Snowball blocks

MATERIALS

24 fat quarters* assorted light shirting prints

24 fat quarters* assorted dark prints in red, blue, black, and gray

1⅝ yards black print for border

¾ yard red print for binding

7½ yards backing fabric

Queen-size quilt batting

*fat quarter = 18" × 20"

Cutting

Measurements include ¼" seam allowances. Border strips are exact length needed. You may want to cut them longer to allow for piecing variations.

From assorted light prints, cut a total of:

• 84 (6½") A squares.

• 336 (2½") B squares.

From assorted dark prints, cut a total of:

• 84 (6½") A squares.

• 336 (2½") B squares.

From black print, cut:

• 9 (6"-wide) strips. Piece strips to make 2 (6" × 84½") side borders and 2 (6" × 83½") top and bottom borders.

From red print, cut:

• 10 (2¼"-wide) strips for binding.

Block Assembly

1. Referring to *Block Assembly Diagrams*, place 1 light print B square atop 1 dark print A square, right sides facing. Stitch diagonally from corner to corner as shown. Trim ¼" beyond stitching. Press open to reveal triangle. Repeat for remaining corners, using matching light print B squares, to complete 1 dark block (*Block Diagrams*). Make 84 dark blocks.

Block Assembly Diagrams

Block Diagrams

2. In the same manner, make 84 light blocks using dark print B squares and light print A squares.

Quilt Assembly

1. Lay out blocks as shown in *Quilt Top Assembly Diagram*. Join into rows; join rows to complete quilt center.

2. Add black print side borders to quilt center. Add black print top and bottom borders to quilt.

Finishing

1. Divide backing into 3 (2½-yard) lengths. Join panels lengthwise. Seams will run horizontally.

2. Layer backing, batting, and quilt top; baste. Quilt as desired. Quilt shown was quilted in the ditch, with a circle in each block, and with overlapping circles in borders *(Quilting Diagram)*.

3. Join 2¼"-wide red print strips into 1 continuous piece for straight-grain French-fold binding. Add binding to quilt.

Quilt Top Assembly Diagram

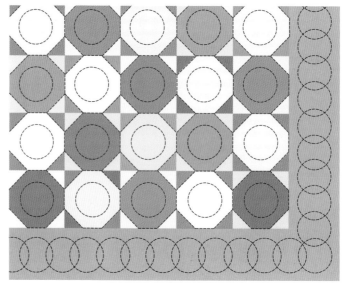

Quilting Diagram

QUILT BY **Lynn Roddy Brown**

Triple Four Patch

Lynn's alternate name for this quilt is Insanity 3044. It started with a bag of triple four patch blocks from a block exchange. Eight quilters each made ten sets of eight identical blocks and then traded them among the group. Lynn added border blocks and sashing to make her version unique.

Size: 68¼" × 81¾"
Blocks: 120 (6") blocks

MATERIALS

7 fat quarters* assorted dark prints
14 fat quarters* assorted medium/dark prints
7 fat quarters* assorted light prints
1¾ yards blue print for border blocks
½ yard gold print for border blocks
¾ yard brown print for binding
¾ yard dark green print for border sashing
1 fat quarter* medium green print for cornerstones
1¼ yards multicolor print for center sashing
5 yards backing fabric
Twin-size quilt batting
*fat quarter = 18" × 20"

Cutting

Measurements include ¼" seam allowances.

From dark print fat quarters, cut a total of:
• 80 (1¼"-wide) strips for strip sets.

From medium/dark print fat quarters, cut a total of:
• 40 (3½"-wide) strips. From strips, cut 80 sets of 2 matching (3½") C squares.
• 40 (2"-wide) strips. From strips, cut 80 sets of 4 matching (2") B squares.

From light print fat quarters, cut a total of:
• 80 (1¼"-wide) strips for strip sets.

From remainders of light print fat quarters, cut a total of:
• 4 (1¼"-wide) strips. From strips, cut 49 (1¼") A squares.

From blue print, cut:
• 8 (3½"-wide) strips. From strips, cut 80 (3½") C squares.
• 8 (2"-wide) strips. From strips, cut 160 (2") B squares.
• 10 (1¼"-wide) strips for strip sets.

From gold print, cut:
• 11 (1¼"-wide) strips. From 1 strip, cut 22 (1¼") A squares. Remaining strips are for strip sets.

From brown print, cut:
• 9 (2¼"-wide) strips for binding.

From dark green print, cut:
• 3 (6½"-wide) strips. From strips, cut 84 (6½" × 1¼") D rectangles.

From medium green print fat quarter, cut:
• 6 (1¼"-wide) strips. From strips, cut 72 (1¼") A squares.

From multicolor print, cut:
• 6 (6½"-wide) strips. From strips, cut 178 (6½" × 1¼") D rectangles.

Block Assembly

1. Join 1 light print strip and 1 dark print strip as shown in *Strip Set Diagram*. Make 80 strip sets. From each strip set, cut 8 (1¼"-wide) segments.

Strip Set Diagram

2. Referring to *Four Patch Unit Diagrams*, join 2 matching segments to make 1 Four Patch Unit. Make 4 matching Four Patch Units.

Four Patch Unit Diagrams

3. Join 2 Four Patch Units and 2 matching B squares as shown in *Double Four Patch Unit Diagrams*. Make 2 Double Four Patch Units.

Double Four Patch Unit Diagrams

4. Lay out Double Four Patch Units and 2 matching C squares as shown in *Block Diagrams*. Join to complete 1 block. Make 80 blocks.

Block Diagrams

Border Block Assembly

1. Join 1 gold print strip and 1 blue print strip as shown in *Strip Set Diagram*. Make 10 strip sets. From strip sets, cut 320 (1¼"-wide) segments.

Strip Set Diagram

2. Join 2 segments as shown in *Four Patch Unit Diagrams*. Make 160 Four Patch Units.

Four Patch Unit Diagrams

3. Join 2 Four Patch Units and 2 blue print B squares as shown in *Double Four Patch Unit Diagrams*. Make 80 Double Four Patch Units.

Double Four Patch Unit Diagrams

4. Lay out 2 Double Four Patch Units and 2 blue print C squares as shown in *Border Block Diagrams*. Join to complete 1 block. Make 40 border blocks.

Border Block Diagrams

Quilt Assembly

1. Lay out blocks, D rectangles, and A squares as shown in *Quilt Top Assembly Diagram* on page 29.

2. Join into rows; join rows to complete quilt top.

> ### Sew Smart™
> Using sashing and cornerstones helps keep the quilt square.
> —Marianne

Finishing

1. Divide backing into 2 (2½-yard) lengths. Cut 1 piece in half lengthwise to make 2 narrow panels. Join 1 narrow panel to each side of wider panel; press seam allowances toward narrow panels.

2. Layer backing, batting, and quilt top; baste. Quilt as desired. Quilt shown was quilted in the ditch around blocks and with allover meandering in blocks (*Quilting Diagram*).

3. Join 2¼"-wide brown print strips into 1 continuous piece for straight-grain French-fold binding. Add binding to quilt.

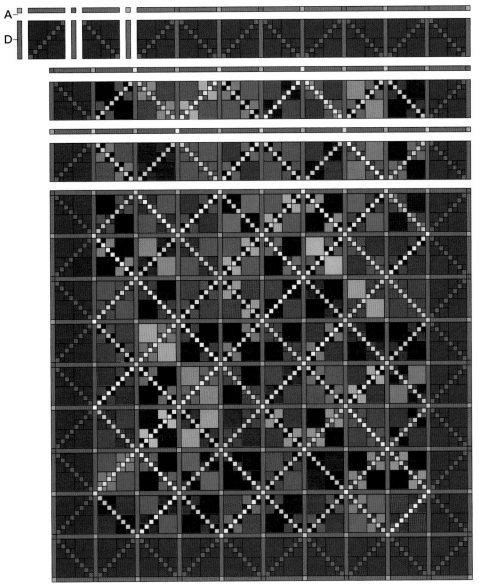

A —
D —

Quilt Top Assembly Diagram

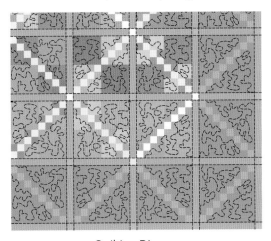

Quilting Diagram

Ko Ko

This quilt is called Ko Ko because it is made of chocolate Shweshwe prints and the name sounds like cocoa. You could also make it using a selection of your favorite reproduction prints.

Size: 45½" × 57"
Blocks: 32 (8") blocks

MATERIALS

10 fat quarters** assorted dark brown prints
16 fat quarters* assorted light prints
½ yard binding fabric
Fons & Porter Half & Quarter Ruler (optional)
3 yards backing fabric
Twin-size quilt batting
**Shweshwe fat quarter = 18″ × 18″
*fat quarter = 18″ × 20″

NOTE: Dark fabrics in the quilt shown are Shweshwe prints from South Africa by Marula Imports.

NOTE: Authentic Shweshwe is 36" wide. It must be washed prior to use to remove excess dye and starch. To read about Shweshwe fabric see page 9.

Cutting

Measurements include ¼" seam allowances. Instructions are written for using the Fons & Porter Half & Quarter Ruler. If not using this ruler follow cutting NOTES.

From each dark print fat quarter, cut:

• 6 (2½"-wide) strips. From strips, cut 52 (2½") half-square A triangles.
  NOTE: If not using the Fons & Porter Half & Quarter Ruler, cut 5 (2⅞"-wide) strips. From strips, cut 26 (2⅞") squares. Cut squares in half diagonally to make 52 half-square A triangles.

From light print fat quarters, cut a total of:

• 4 (12⅝"-wide) strips. From strips, cut 4 (12⅝") squares. Cut squares in half diagonally in both directions to make 16 side setting triangles (2 are extra).
• 2 (6⅝"-wide) strips. From strips, cut 2 (6⅝") squares. Cut squares in half diagonally to make 4 corner setting triangles.
• 52 (2½"-wide) strips. From strips, cut 512 (2½") half-square A triangles.
  NOTE: If not using the Fons & Porter Half & Quarter Ruler, cut 52 (2⅞"-wide) strips. From strips, cut 256 (2⅞") squares. Cut squares in half diagonally to make 512 half-square A triangles.

From binding fabric, cut:

• 6 (2¼"-wide) strips for binding.

Block Assembly

1. Join 1 dark print A triangle and 1 light print A triangle as shown in *Triangle-Square Diagrams*. Make 512 triangle-squares.

Triangle-Square Diagrams

2. Lay out 16 triangle-squares as shown in *Block Assembly Diagram*. Join into rows; join rows to complete 1 block *(Block Diagram)*. Make 32 blocks.

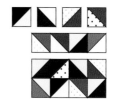

Block Assembly Diagram

Block Diagram

Quilt Assembly

1. Lay out blocks and setting triangles as shown in *Quilt Top Assembly Diagram*.

2. Join into diagonal rows; join rows to complete quilt top.

Finishing

1. Divide backing into 2 (1½-yard) lengths. Join panels lengthwise. Seam will run horizontally.

Quilt Top Assembly Diagram

2. Layer backing, batting, and quilt top; baste. Quilt as desired. Quilt shown was quilted with small meandering *(Quilting Diagram)*.

3. Join 2¼"-wide light print strips into 1 continuous piece for straight-grain French-fold binding. Add binding to quilt.

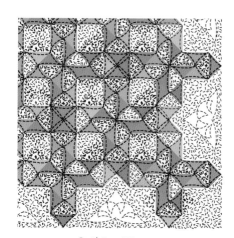

Quilting Diagram

Scrappy Triangles

Jean Nolte's quilt began as a scrappy triangle-square exchange with a dozen friends. She used a teal batik for the sashing, borders, and binding to tie it all together.

Size: 62" × 79"

Blocks: 12 (16") blocks

MATERIALS

18 fat quarters** or 36 fat eighths* assorted dark prints

19 fat quarters** or 38 fat eighths* assorted light prints

2¼ yards teal print for sashing, border, and binding

36 Laundry Basket Quilts Half-Square Triangle Exchange Papers (optional)

Fons & Porter Quarter Inch Seam Marker (optional)

4¾ yards backing fabric

Twin-size quilt batting

*fat eighth = 9" × 20"

**fat quarter = 18" × 20"

Cutting

Measurements include ¼" seam allowances.

NOTE: Instructions are written using Half-Square Triangle Exchange Paper cut into smaller sections. This will make more combinations of prints for a scrappier look. Another option is to use the Fons & Porter Quarter Inch Seam Marker to make triangle-squares. See *Quick Triangle-Squares* on page 61 for instructions. If not using triangle papers or Quarter Inch Seam Marker, make 2"-finished triangle-squares using your preferred method.

From assorted dark prints, cut a total of:

• 36 (6⅛"-wide) strips. From strips, cut 108 (6⅛") A squares.

From assorted light prints, cut a total of:

• 36 (6⅛"-wide) strips. From strips, cut 108 (6⅛") A squares.

• 18 (2½"-wide) strips. From strips, cut 144 (2½") B squares.

• 20 (1½") sashing squares.

From teal print, cut:

• 4 (2¼"-wide) **lengthwise** strips for binding.

• 13 (1½"-wide**) lengthwise** strips. From strips, cut 2 (1½" × 77½") side outer borders, 2 (1½" × 62½") top and bottom outer borders, 31 (1½" × 16½") long sashing strips, and 18 (1½" × 4½") short sashing strips.

Triangle-Squares

1. Cut triangle papers into 108 sections of 4 squares each. Layer 1 light print A square atop 1 dark print A square, right sides facing. Place 1 paper square atop pair of squares; pin in place.

Sew Smart™

Seam allowance of the triangle-squares will all automatically go toward the dark fabric when pressed if the paper is placed on the light fabric. —Liz

2. Stitch on dashed lines as shown in *Stitching Diagram*. Cut on all solid lines, including outer lines, to make 8 triangle-squares. With paper still attached, press seam allowances of triangle-squares toward dark fabric. Repeat to make a total of 864 triangle-squares. Carefully remove paper from triangle-squares.

Stitching Diagram

Block Assembly

1. Lay out 13 triangle-squares and 3 light print B squares as shown in *Quadrant Diagram*. Join into rows; join rows to complete 1 quadrant. Make 4 quadrants.

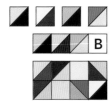

Quadrant Diagram

2. Lay out 4 quadrants as shown in *Block Assembly Diagram*. Join into rows; join rows to complete 1 block (*Block Diagram*). Make 12 blocks.

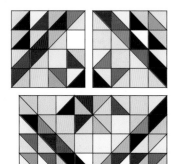

Block Assembly Diagram

Block Diagram

Border Unit Assembly

1. Lay out 16 triangle-squares as shown in *Border Unit Assembly Diagram*. Join into rows; join rows to complete 1 Border Unit (*Border Unit Diagram*). Make 14 Border Units.

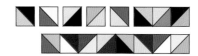

Border Unit Assembly Diagram

Border Unit Diagram

2. Lay out 4 triangle-squares as shown in *Corner Unit Assembly Diagram*. Join into rows; join rows to complete 1 Corner Unit (*Corner Unit Diagram*). Make 4 Corner Units.

Corner Unit Assembly Diagram

Corner Unit Diagram

Quilt Assembly

1. Lay out blocks, sashing strips, sashing squares, Border Units, and Corner Units as shown in *Quilt Top Assembly Diagram*.

2. Join into rows; join rows to complete quilt center.

3. Add teal print side outer borders to quilt center. Add top and bottom outer borders to quilt.

Finishing

1. Divide backing into 2 (2⅜-yard) lengths. Cut 1 piece in half lengthwise to make 2 narrow panels. Join 1 narrow panel to each side of wider panel. Press seam allowances toward narrow panels.

2. Layer backing, batting, and quilt top; baste. Quilt as desired. Quilt shown was quilted in the ditch and with a diamond pattern in the background of the stars (*Quilting Diagram*).

3. Join 2¼"-wide teal print strips into 1 continuous piece for straight-grain French-fold binding. Add binding to quilt.

Quilting Diagram

Quilt Top Assembly Diagram

Triangle Surprise

What a great way to use scraps! Designer Edyta Sitar used batiks, homespuns, reproductions, shirtings, and contemporary prints all together in this appealing quilt.

Size: 56" × 56"
Blocks: 49 (8") blocks

MATERIALS

17 fat quarters* assorted light prints
17 fat quarters* assorted dark prints
½ yard teal print for binding
8 Laundry Basket Quilts Half-Square
    Triangle Exchange Papers (optional)
3½ yards backing fabric
Twin-size quilt batting
*fat quarter = 18" × 20"

Cutting

Measurements include ¼" seam allowances. Border strips are exact length needed. You may want to make them longer to allow for piecing variations.

NOTE: Instructions are written using Half-Square Triangle Exchange Paper cut into smaller sections. This will make more combinations of prints for a scrappier look. If not using these papers, make 2"-finished triangle-squares using your preferred method.

From each light fat quarter, cut:
• 1 (6⅛"-wide) strip. From strip, cut 3 (6⅛") B squares.
• 1 (2⅞"-wide) strip. From strip, cut 6 (2⅞") squares. Cut squares in half diagonally to make 12 half-square A triangles.

From each dark fat quarter, cut:
• 1 (6⅛"-wide) strip. From strip, cut 3 (6⅛") B squares.
• 1 (2⅞"-wide) strip. From strip, cut 6 (2⅞") squares. Cut squares in half diagonally to make 12 half-square A triangles.

From teal print, cut:
• 7 (2¼"-wide) strips for binding.

Block Assembly

1. Cut triangle papers into 25 sections of 4 squares each. Layer 1 light print B square atop 1 dark print B square, right sides facing. Place 1 paper square atop pair of squares; pin in place.

Sew Smart™

Seam allowance of the triangle-square will automatically go toward the dark fabric when the paper is placed on the light fabric. —Liz

2. Stitch on dashed lines as shown in *Stitching Diagram* on page 40. Cut

on all solid lines, including outer lines, to make 8 triangle-squares. With paper still attached, press seam allowances of triangle-squares toward dark fabric. Repeat to make a total of 196 triangle-squares. Carefully remove paper from triangle-squares.

Stitching Diagram

3. Join 1 triangle-square and 2 dark print A triangles as shown in *Corner Unit Diagrams*. Make 100 dark Corner Units.

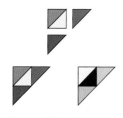

Corner Unit Diagrams

4. In the same manner, join 1 triangle-square and 2 light print A triangles to complete 1 light Corner Unit. Make 96 light Corner Units.

5. Lay out 4 dark Corner Units and 1 light print B square as shown in *Light Block Assembly Diagram*. Join to complete 1 light block *(Light Block Diagram)*. Make 25 light blocks.

Light Block Assembly Diagram

Light Block Diagram

6. Referring to *Dark Block Assembly Diagram*, join 4 light Corner Units and 1 dark print B square to complete 1 dark block *(Dark Block Diagram)*. Make 24 dark blocks.

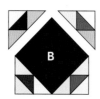

Dark Block Assembly Diagram

Dark Block Diagram

Quilt Assembly

1. Lay out blocks as shown in *Quilt Top Assembly Diagram*.

2. Join into rows; join rows to complete quilt top.

Finishing

1. Divide backing into 2 (1¾-yard) lengths. Cut 1 piece in half lengthwise to make 2 narrow panels. Join 1 narrow panel to wider panel; press seam allowances toward narrow panel. Remaining panel is extra and can be used to make a hanging sleeve.

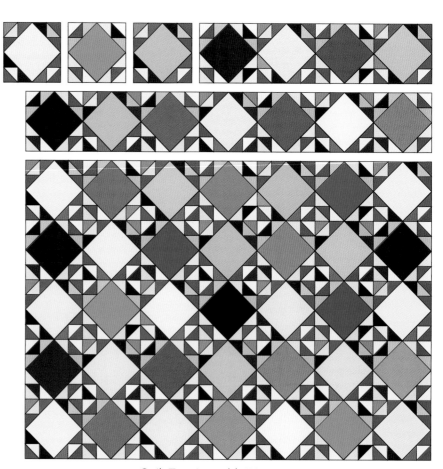

Quilt Top Assembly Diagram

2. Layer backing, batting, and quilt top; baste. Quilt as desired. Quilt shown was quilted with an allover design *(Quilting Diagram)*.

3. Join 2¼"-wide teal print strips into 1 continuous piece for straight-grain French-fold binding. Add binding to quilt.

Quilting Diagram

QUILT BY **Ashley Newcomb**

Trail Marker

Colorful arrows point the way left and right. Which way to go?
How about right into a comfy chair with a good book and this quilt?

Size: 56" × 65"

Blocks: 104 (5" × 7") blocks

MATERIALS

16 fat quarters* assorted prints in
  turquoise, green, orange, gray, and
  brown

1 yard each of 8 assorted solids in
  white, tan, and gray

Template material

⅝ yard turquoise print for binding

3½ yards backing fabric

Twin-size quilt batting

*fat quarter = 18" × 20"

Cutting

Measurements include ¼" seam
allowances. Pattern for A triangle is
on page 45.

From fat quarters, cut a total of:

• 104 A triangles.

From each solid yard, cut:

• 3 (10"-wide) strips. From strips,
  cut 13 (10" × 8") rectangles. Cut
  rectangles in half diagonally to
  make 26 B triangles.

NOTE: If using print fabrics, cut
half of the rectangles in half from
lower left to upper right and cut
half of the rectangles in half from
lower right to upper left (*Cutting
Diagrams*).

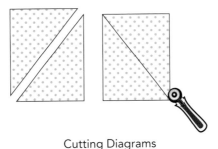

Cutting Diagrams

From turquoise print, cut:

• 7 (2¼"-wide) strips for binding.

Block Assembly

1. Join 1 print A triangle and 1 solid
   B triangle as shown in *Block
   Assembly Diagrams*. Trim B triangle
   even with edge of A triangle as
   shown.

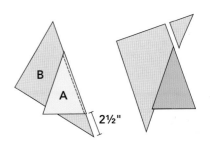

2½"

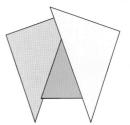

Block Assembly Diagrams

2. Add 1 solid B triangle to opposite side of A triangle.

3. Trim block to (5½" × 7½") to complete 1 block *(Block Diagram)*. Make 104 blocks.

Block Diagram

Sew Smart™

If not using ruler and rotary cutter to trim block, place (5½" × 7½") plastic template rectangle atop block; draw around template. Cut on drawn line. —Marianne

Quilt Assembly

1. Lay out blocks as shown in *Quilt Top Assembly Diagram.*

2. Join into rows; join rows to complete quilt top.

Finishing

1. Divide backing into 2 (1¾-yard) lengths. Join panels lengthwise. Seam will run horizontally.

2. Layer backing, batting, and quilt top; baste. Quilt as desired. Quilt shown was quilted with straight lines *(Quilting Diagram).*

3. Join 2¼"-wide turquoise print strips into 1 continuous piece for straight-grain French-fold binding. Add binding to quilt.

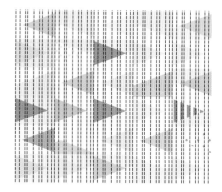

Quilting Diagram

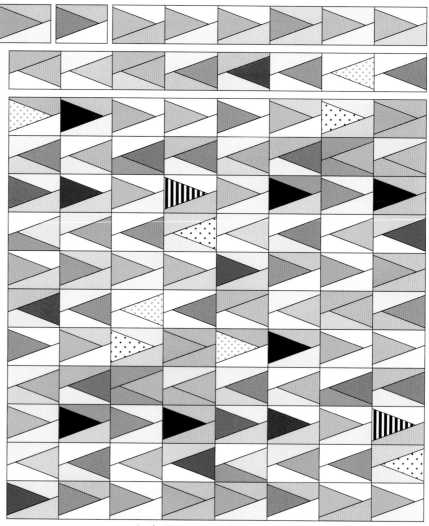

Quilt Top Assembly Diagram

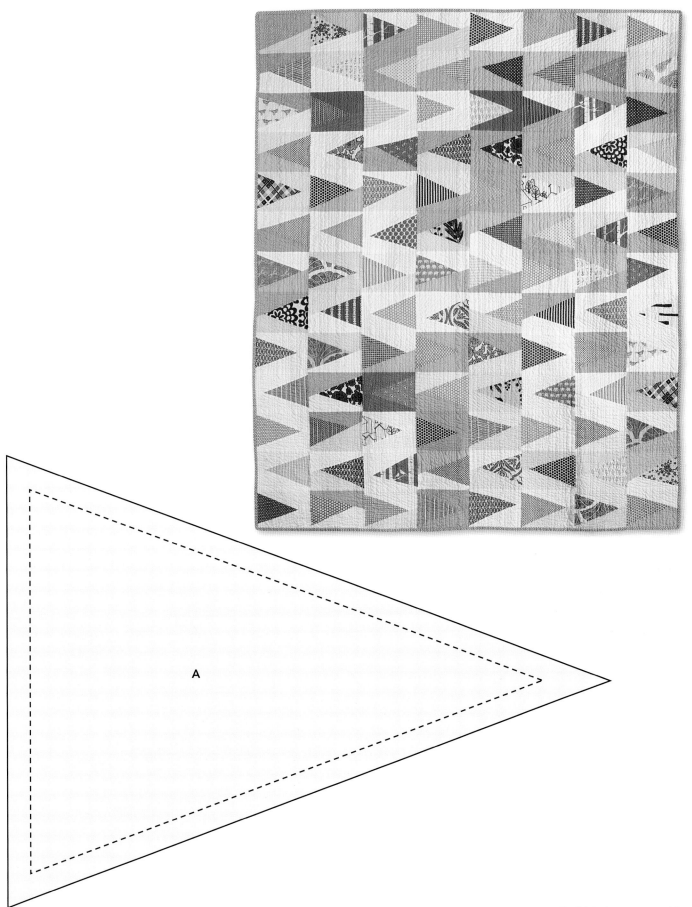

A

QUILT DESIGNED AND MADE BY **Liz Porter**

HAND QUILTED BY THE **Ada Troyer Family**

Barbed Wire

Liz says, "I used lots of my small scraps to make this zigzag quilt. The black print background perfectly highlights the many colors in the triangles."

Size: 56½" × 85"

Blocks: 155 (4") Four Patch Units

MATERIALS

9 fat quarters** or 18 fat eighths* assorted light prints

9 fat quarters** or 18 fat eighths* assorted dark prints

2¾ yards black print for background

⅝ yard red print for binding

Fons & Porter Half & Quarter Ruler (optional)

5¼ yards backing fabric

Twin-size quilt batting

*fat eighth = 9" × 20"

**fat quarter = 18" × 20"

Cutting

Measurements include ¼" seam allowances. Instructions are written for using the Fons & Porter Half & Quarter Ruler. If not using this ruler, follow cutting NOTES.

From assorted light prints, cut a total of:

• 52 (2½"-wide) strips. From strips, cut 620 half-square triangles.

  NOTE: If not using the Fons & Porter Half & Quarter Ruler, cut 52 (2⅞"-wide) strips. From strips, cut 310 (2⅞") squares. Cut squares in half diagonally to make 620 half-square triangles.

From assorted dark prints, cut a total of:

• 52 (2½"-wide) strips. From strips, cut 620 half-square triangles.

  NOTE: If not using the Fons & Porter Half & Quarter Ruler, cut 52 (2⅞"-wide) strips. From strips, cut 310 (2⅞") squares. Cut squares in half diagonally to make 620 half-square triangles.

From black print, cut:

• 21 (4½"-wide) strips. From strips, cut 40 (4½" × 12½") A rectangles, 8 (4½" × 8½") B rectangles, and 42 (4½") C squares.

From red print, cut:

• 8 (2¼"-wide) strips for binding.

ZigZag Unit Assembly

1. Join 1 light print triangle and 1 dark print triangle as shown in *Triangle-Square Diagrams*. Make 620 triangle-squares.

Triangle-Square Diagrams

2. Join 4 triangle-squares as shown in *Four Patch Unit Diagrams*. Make 155 Four Patch Units.

Four Patch Unit Diagrams

3. Join 4 Four Patch Units, 1 black print A rectangle, and 1 black print C square as shown in *Unit 1 Diagrams*. Make 30 Unit 1.

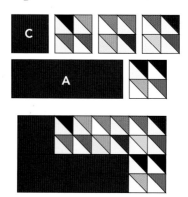

Unit 1 Diagrams

4. Join 4 Four Patch Units and 1 black print A rectangle as shown in *Unit 2 Diagrams*. Make 5 Unit 2.

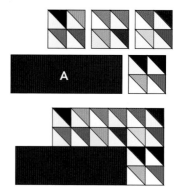

Unit 2 Diagrams

5. Join 3 Four Patch Units, 1 black print A rectangle, and 1 black print C square as shown in *Unit 3 Diagrams*. Make 5 Unit 3.

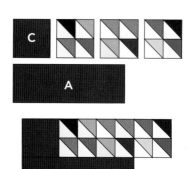

Unit 3 Diagrams

Quilt Assembly

1. Lay out Units 1, 2, and 3, black print B rectangles, and remaining black print C squares as shown in *Quilt Top Assembly Diagram*.

2. Join into diagonal rows; join rows.

3. Trim sides of quilt ¼" beyond points of outer Four Patch units as shown in *Quilt Top Assembly Diagram*. Trim top and bottom of quilt ¼" beyond inner points as shown to complete quilt top.

Quilt Top Assembly Diagram

Finishing

1. Divide backing into 2 (2⅝-yard) lengths. Cut 1 piece in half lengthwise to make 2 narrow panels. Join 1 narrow panel to each side of wider panel; press seam allowances toward narrow panels.

2. Layer backing, batting, and quilt top; baste. Quilt as desired. Quilt shown was hand quilted inside each triangle and with a feather design in background *(Quilting Diagram)*.

3. Join 2¼"-wide red print strips into 1 continuous piece for straight-grain French-fold binding. Add binding to quilt.

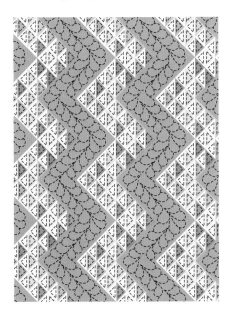

Quilting Diagram

QUILT BY **Jean Nolte**

Snow Geese

A flock of geese flies across a snowy arctic landscape. Calm and sophisticated, this quilt helps you perfect your piecing skills and is sure to fly right in your home!

Size: 69" × 75"

MATERIALS

14 fat quarters* assorted blue and gray prints for Flying Geese Units
6 yards white solid for Flying Geese Units, sashing, and binding
4¼ yards backing fabric
Twin-size quilt batting
*fat quarter = 18" × 20"

Cutting

Measurements include ¼" seam allowances. Sashing strips are exact length needed. You may want to make them longer to allow for piecing variations.

From assorted blue and gray print fat quarters, cut a total of:

• 32 (3½"-wide) strips. From strips cut 94 (3½" × 6½") A rectangles.

From white solid, cut:

• 6 (6½"-wide) strips. From strips, cut 8 (6½" × 3½") A rectangles, 1 (6½" × 33½") H rectangle, 1 (6½" × 24½") G rectangle, 1 (6½" × 18½") F rectangle, 1 (6½" × 12½") E rectangle, 1 (6½" × 9½") D rectangle, and 8 (6½") C squares.
• 18 (3½"-wide) strips. From strips, cut 188 (3½") B squares.
• 8 (2¼"-wide) strips for binding.

From remainder of white solid, cut:

• 1 (13½"-wide) **lengthwise** strip. From strip, cut 1 (13½" × 75½") N sashing strip.
• 1 (8½"-wide) **lengthwise** strip. From strip, cut 1 (8½" × 75½") M sashing strip.
• 1 (5½"-wide) **lengthwise** strip. From strip, cut 1 (5½" × 75½") L sashing strip.
• 1 (3½"-wide) **lengthwise** strip. From strip, cut 1 (3½" × 75½") K sashing strip.
• 1 (2½"-wide) **lengthwise** strip. From strip, cut 1 (2½" × 75½") J sashing strip.
• 2 (1½"-wide) **lengthwise** strips. From strips, cut 2 (1½" × 75½") I sashing strips.

Flying Geese Assembly

1. Referring to *Flying Geese Unit Diagrams*, place 1 white print B square atop 1 print A rectangle, right sides facing. Stitch diagonally from corner to corner as shown. Trim ¼" beyond stitching. Press open to reveal triangle. Repeat for opposite end of rectangle to complete 1 Flying Geese Unit. Make 94 Flying Geese Units.

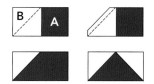

Flying Geese Unit Diagrams

Quilt Assembly

1. Lay out Flying Geese Units and white A, D, E, F, G, and H rectangles and C squares as shown in *Quilt Top Assembly Diagram*. Join to make vertical rows.

2. Layout rows and sashing strips. Join to complete quilt center.

Finishing

1. Divide backing into 2 (2⅛-yard) lengths. Join panels lengthwise. Seam will run horizontally.

2. Layer backing, batting, and quilt top; baste. Quilt as desired. Quilt shown was quilted in a zigzag pattern *(Quilting Diagram)*.

3. Join 2¼"-wide white strips into 1 continuous piece for straight-grain French-fold binding. Add binding to quilt.

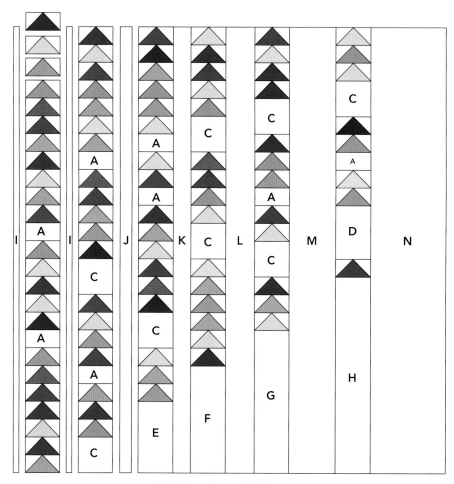

Quilt Top Assembly Diagram

Quilting Diagram

QUILT BY **Nancy Mahoney**

Spin City

Here's a modern twist using an appealing variety of 1930s reproduction prints.
This quilt brings new life to a traditional design.

Size: 50" × 58"

Blocks: 30 (8") blocks

MATERIALS

21 fat quarters* assorted prints for
   blocks and pieced border

1⅝ yards white solid for blocks and
   inner border

½ yard brown print for binding

Tri-Recs™ Tools or template material

3¼ yards backing fabric

Twin-size quilt batting

*fat quarter = 18" × 20"

Cutting

Measurements include ¼" seam
allowances. Border strips are exact
length needed. You may want to make
them longer to allow for piecing
variations. Patterns for A and B
triangles are on page 57.

> **Sew Smart**™
>
> **Use the Tri-Recs™ Tools to make
> quick work of cutting A and B tri-
> angles. Refer to the instructions
> on page 62. —Liz**

**From assorted fat quarters, cut a
total of:**

- 92 (4½" × 2½") C rectangles.
- 16 (2½") D squares.
- 30 sets of 4 matching A triangles.

From white solid, cut:

- 5 (1½"-wide) strips. Piece strips to
  make 2 (1½" × 48½") side inner
  borders and 2 (1½" × 42½") top
  and bottom inner borders.
- 10 (4½"-wide) strips. From strips,
  cut 120 B triangles and 120 B
  triangles reversed.

> **Sew Smart**™
>
> **Stack strips with wrong sides
> facing to cut B and B reversed
> triangles at the same time.
> —Marianne**

From brown print, cut:

- 6 (2¼"-wide) strips for binding.

Block Assembly

1. Join 1 print A triangle, 1 white B triangle, and 1 white B triangle reversed as shown in *Block Unit Diagrams*. Make 4 matching Block Units.

Block Unit Diagrams

2. Lay out Block Units as shown in *Block Assembly Diagram*. Join into rows; join rows to complete 1 block *(Block Diagram)*. Make 30 blocks.

Block Assembly Diagram

Block Diagram

Border Assembly

1. Join 4 print D squares as shown in *Four Patch Unit Diagrams*. Make 4 Four Patch Units.

Four Patch Unit Diagrams

2. Referring to *Quilt Top Assembly Diagram*, join 25 C rectangles to make pieced side border. Make 2 pieced side borders.

3. In the same manner, make pieced top border using 21 C rectangles and 2 Four Patch Units.

4. Repeat for pieced bottom border.

Quilt Assembly

1. Lay out blocks as shown in *Quilt Top Assembly Diagram*.

2. Join blocks into rows; join rows to complete quilt center.

3. Add white side inner borders to quilt center. Add white top and bottom inner borders to quilt.

4. Repeat for pieced outer borders.

Finishing

1. Divide backing into 2 (1⅝-yard) lengths. Join panels lengthwise. Seam will run horizontally.

2. Layer backing, batting, and quilt top; baste. Quilt as desired. Quilt shown was quilted with an allover swirl design *(Quilting Diagram)*.

3. Join 2¼"-wide brown print strips into 1 continuous piece for straight-grain French-fold binding. Add binding to quilt.

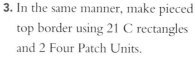

Quilt Top Assembly Diagram

Quilting Diagram

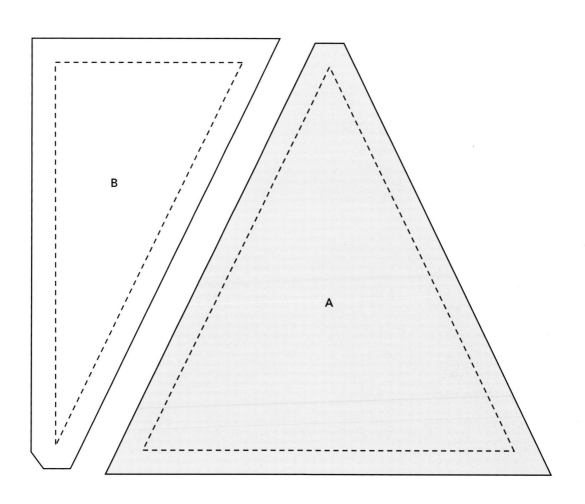

Basic Supplies

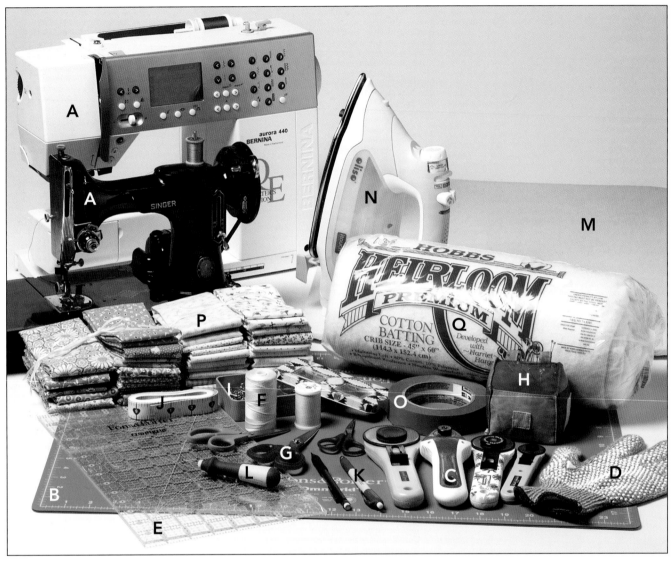

You'll need a **sewing machine (A)** in good working order to construct patchwork blocks, join blocks together, add borders, and machine quilt. We encourage you to purchase a machine from a local dealer, who can help you with service in the future, rather than from a discount store. Another option may be to borrow a machine from a friend or family member. If the machine has not been used in a while, have it serviced by a local dealer to make sure it is in good working order. If you need an extension cord, one with a surge protector is a good idea.

A **rotary cutting mat (B)** is essential for accurate and safe rotary cutting. Purchase one that is no smaller than 18" × 24". Rotary cutting mats are made of "self-healing" material that can be used over and over.

A **rotary cutter (C)** is a cutting tool that looks like a pizza cutter, and has a very sharp blade. We recommend starting with a standard size 45mm rotary cutter. Always lock or close your cutter when it is not in use, and keep it out of the reach of children.

A **safety glove** (also known as a *Klutz Glove)* **(D)** is also recommended. Wear your safety glove on the hand that is holding the ruler in place. Because it is made of cut-resistant material, the safety glove protects your non-cutting hand from accidents that can occur if your cutting hand slips while cutting.

An acrylic **ruler (E)** is used in combination with your cutting mat and rotary cutter. We recommend the Fons & Porter 8" × 14" ruler, but a 6" × 12" ruler is another good option. You'll need a ruler with inch, quarter-inch, and eighth-inch markings that show clearly for ease of measuring. Choose a ruler with 45-degree-angle, 30-degree-angle, and 60-degree-angle lines marked on it as well.

Since you will be using 100% cotton fabric for your quilts, use **cotton or cotton-covered polyester thread (F)** for piecing and quilting. Avoid 100% polyester thread, as it tends to snarl.

Keep a pair of small **scissors (G)** near your sewing machine for cutting threads.

Thin, good-quality **straight pins (H)** are preferred by quilters. The

pins included with pincushions are normally too thick to use for piecing, so discard them. Purchase a box of nickel-plated brass **safety pins** size #1 **(I)** to use for pin-basting the layers of your quilt together for machine quilting.

Invest in a 120"-long dressmaker's **measuring tape (J)**. This will come in handy when making borders for your quilt.

A 0.7–0.9mm mechanical **pencil (K)** works well for marking on your fabric.

Invest in a quality, sharp **seam ripper (L)**. Every quilter gets well acquainted with her seam ripper!

Set up an **ironing board (M)** and **iron (N)** in your sewing area. Pressing yardage before cutting, and pressing patchwork seams as you go are both essential for quality quiltmaking. Select an iron that has steam capability.

Masking **tape (O)** or painter's tape works well to mark your sewing machine so you can sew an accurate ¼" seam. You will also use tape to hold your backing fabric taut as you prepare your quilt sandwich for machine quilting.

The most exciting item that you will need for quilting is **fabric (P)**. Quilters generally prefer 100% cotton fabrics for their quilts. This fabric is woven from cotton threads, and has

a lengthwise and a crosswise grain. The term "bias" is used to describe the diagonal grain of the fabric. If you make a 45-degree angle cut through a square of cotton fabric, the cut edges will be bias edges, which are quite stretchy. As you learn more quiltmaking techniques, you'll learn how bias can work to your advantage or disadvantage.

Fabric is sold by the yard at quilt shops and fabric stores. Quilting fabric is generally about 40"–44" wide, so a yard is about 40" wide by 36" long. As you collect fabrics to build your own personal stash, you will buy yards, half yards (about 18" × 40"), quarter yards (about 9" × 40"), as well as other lengths.

Many quilt shops sell "fat quarters," a special cut favored by quilters. A fat quarter is created by cutting a half yard down the fold line into two 18" × 20" pieces (fat quarters) that are sold separately. Quilters like the nearly square shape of the fat quarter because it is more useful than the narrow regular quarter yard cut.

Batting (Q) is the filler between quilt top and backing that makes your quilt a quilt. It can be cotton, polyester, cotton-polyester blend, wool, silk, or other natural materials, such as bamboo or corn. Make sure the batting you buy is at least six inches wider and six inches longer than your quilt top.

SEW easy™ Techniques

Strip Sets

A strip set is a group of strips that are sewn together lengthwise in a particular sequence. Completed strip sets are later cut into smaller segments to use as blocks or portions of blocks.

NOTE: Perfectly straight and accurately cut strips are essential for strip sets. If strips are cut across folded width of fabric, open strips to see that they are straight. If strips are not cut exactly perpendicular to fold, they will bow where they were folded, making a crooked strip.

1. To make a strip set, pair two strips with right sides facing and raw edges aligned. Machine stitch with ¼" seam. Press seam to one side. Begin by pressing strips flat, just as you have sewn them, to set stitching *(Photo A)*.

    Fold top fabric strip back, revealing right side of seam and strip set. Gently, with side of iron, press seam open on right side with seam allowances to one side *(Photo B)*. Strip set should be straight, without any distortion along outside edges.

2. Add third strip to complete strip set. If making strip sets with more than three strips, join strips in pairs and then sew pairs together. Make required number of strip sets.

Sew Smart™
Pinning strip edges in a few places will help prevent bottom strip in pair from drawing up. Alternating sewing direction from strip to strip will help keep strip sets straight.
—Liz

3. Aligning horizontal lines on ruler with long edge and seam lines of strip set, trim uneven end of strip set.

4. Keeping horizontal lines on ruler aligned with strip set, cut required width segments *(Photo C)*. Cut required number of strip set segments.

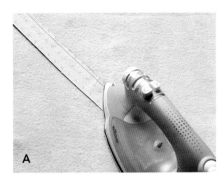

A

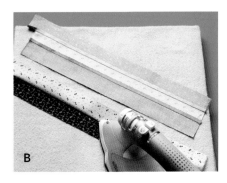

B

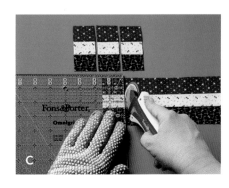

C

SEW easy™

Quick Triangle-Squares

Use this quick technique to make triangle-squares.
The Fons & Porter Quarter Inch Seam Marker offers a neat way
to mark accurate sewing lines for this method.

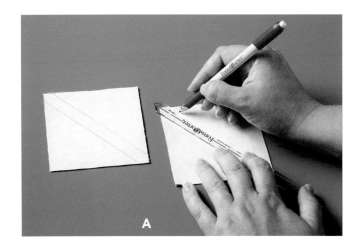

1. From each of 2 fabrics, cut 1 square ⅞" larger than the desired finished size of the triangle-square. For example, to make a triangle-square that will finish 2", cut 2⅞" squares.

2. On wrong side of lighter square, place the Quarter Inch Seam Marker diagonally across the square, with the yellow center line positioned exactly at opposite corners. Mark stitching lines along both sides of the Quarter Inch Seam Marker *(Photo A)*.

3. Place light square atop darker square, right sides facing; stitch along both marked sewing lines.

4. Cut between rows of stitching to make 2 triangle-squares *(Photo B)*.

SEW easy™

Using Tri-Recs™ Tools

Three-triangle units were nicknamed "Peaky and Spike" by quilter Doreen Speckmann, who used these units extensively in her quilts. The larger, central triangle is "Spike," and the smaller, side triangle is "Peaky." Follow our instructions for using the Tri-Recs™ tools to make cutting and piecing these units a snap.

Cutting "Peaky and Spike" Triangles

1. Begin by cutting 1 fabric strip from each of the colors you wish to combine in a "Peaky and Spike" unit. To determine the strip size, add ½" to the desired finished size of the unit. For example, for a 4" finished unit, cut strips 4½" wide.

2. Working with the strip for the center "Spike" triangle, position the Tri tool atop the strip, aligning the mark corresponding to your strip width along bottom edge of strip. Cut along both angled sides of Tri tool *(Photo A)*.

3. Reposition Tri tool with strip width line along top edge of strip and side along previously cut edge. Cut another "Spike" triangle *(Photo B)*. Continue in this manner to cut desired number of "Spike" triangles.

4. Fold the strip for the side "Peaky" triangles in half with right sides together so you will be cutting two mirror image pieces at one time. Position the Recs tool atop the strip, aligning the mark corresponding to your strip width along bottom edge of strip. Cut on both sides of Recs tool to cut 2 "Peaky" triangles—1 right and 1 left *(Photo C)*.

5. Reposition Recs tool with strip width line along top

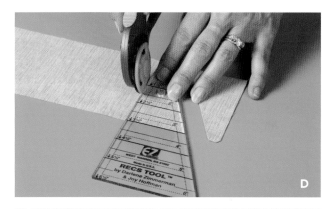

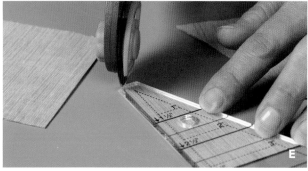

edge of strip. Cut 2 more side "Peaky" triangles (Photo D). Continue in this manner to cut desired number of pairs of "Peaky" triangles.

6. As you cut "Peaky" triangles, be sure to trim along the short angled line at the top of the Recs tool. This angled cut makes it easier to align pieces for sewing (Photo E).

Assembling "Peaky and Spike" Units

1. Position right "Peaky" triangle along right side of "Spike" triangle, making sure the angle aligns with the side of the "Spike" triangle. Join pieces (Photo F). Open out "Peaky" triangle; press seam allowances toward "Peaky" triangle.

2. Add left "Peaky" triangle to adjacent side as shown (Photo G).

3. Open out "Peaky" triangle; press seam allowances toward "Peaky" triangle (Photo H).

4. Trim points of seam allowances even with sides of "Peaky and Spike" unit (Photo I).

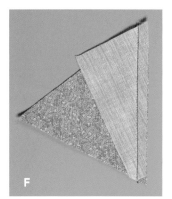

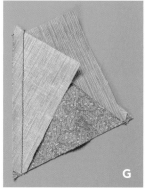

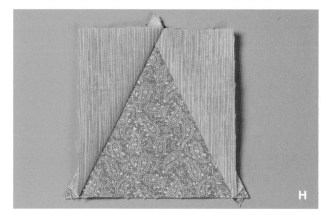

SEW easy™

Cutting Half-Square and Quarter-Square Triangles

With the Fons & Porter Half & Quarter Ruler, you can easily cut half-square and quarter-square triangles from strips of the same width.

Cutting Half-Square Triangles

1. Straighten the left edge of fabric strip. Place the line of the Fons & Porter Half & Quarter Ruler that corresponds with your strip width on the bottom edge of strip, aligning left edge of ruler with straightened edge of strip. The yellow tip of ruler will extend beyond top edge of strip.

2. Cut along right edge of ruler to make 1 half-square triangle *(Photo A)*.

3. Turn ruler and align same line with top edge of strip. Cut along right edge of ruler *(Photo B)*.

4. Repeat to cut required number of half-square triangles.

Cutting Quarter-Square Triangles

1. Place Fons & Porter Half & Quarter Ruler on fabric strip, with line that corresponds with your strip width along bottom edge. The black tip of ruler will extend beyond top edge. Trim off end of strip along left edge of ruler.

2. Cut along right edge of ruler to make 1 quarter-square triangle *(Photo C)*.

3. Turn ruler and align same line along top edge of strip. Cut along right edge of ruler *(Photo D)*.

4. Repeat to cut required number of quarter-square triangles.

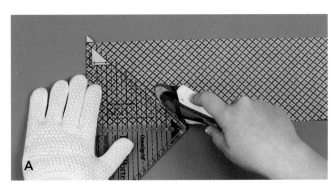

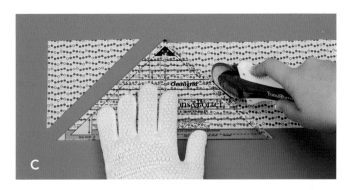

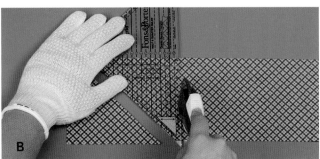

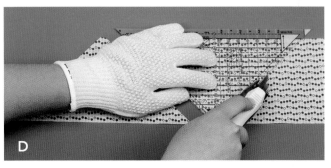